Iowa's Best

MW01609922

An Anthology

Compiled and Edited by
Z Publishing House

2018

Table of Contents

4

5

Foreword, or How This Series Came to Be

There is a troubling catch-22 that exists in the world of publishing: in order to be published—at least by any of the major houses—you must already have been published. The logic works like this: Publishing houses want to sell books. What easier way to sell books than by publishing authors who already have amassed large followings of readers to whom they can market? Inevitably, this cycle leaves the aspiring author with the pressing question of where to begin. Sure, the dramatic rise of self-publishing platforms has enabled everyone to put their writing out there, which is great, but it does come with its own set of problems. Namely, when everyone actually does put their writing out there, as has happened, the question now becomes: Where are the readers to begin? With the oversaturation of the market, readers could spend entire lifetimes buying and reading self-published books and still not find that one author with whom they truly resonate. On Amazon alone, for instance, a new book is uploaded every five minutes, and that number is only set to rise as more and more people take advantage of the self-empowering platforms available to writers today.

The good news is that readers want to discover new talent. This we learned firsthand after beginning Z Publishing in November of 2015. What started as a small Facebook group designed to bring independent writers together on a shared platform of exposure soon transcended into a wave of newfound appreciation for independent writing. Within a few short months, Z Publishing had amassed tens of thousands of followers across social media. Once we knew the idea had struck a chord with a growing group of people, we took the next step and launched Z Publishing's own website in March of 2016. Publishing articles from writers of a multitude of genres—including travel, fiction, politics, lifestyle, and, of course, poetry—the website garnished more support from readers and writers alike, and our following continued to grow.

Though writers of several genres contributed greatly in the early months following Z Publishing's launch, the tremendous support from the poets in particular convinced us that Z Publishing's mission was an idea worth pursuing. We began to receive hundreds of submissions from poets across social media. Many of whom thanked us personally for the extra exposure. In fact, we should have been thanking them, the creators of the great content that had brought the readers to Z Publishing in the first place. Regardless, the poets displayed a level of support for Z Publishing that we never could have expected, and so when we decided it was time to take the next step in Z Publishing's evolution and publish our first official book, we knew exactly who to turn to.

Even though we had high expectations, the result of Z Publishing's first book publishing attempt was truly surprising: Fifty talented poets, from sixteen countries, all worked with enthusiasm to produce a volume of independent poetry that could appeal to all readers of poetry, and Z Poetry: An Anthology of International Indie Poetry (Volume 1) was proudly published in August of 2016, officially marking our status as a book publisher.

Since that time, we've produced and published books in numerous genres, but we've never lost sight of our poetry roots. From state poets laureate to poets who have never before been published, we've continued to promote the work of talented wordsmiths across the globe. In our eyes, anyone who produces good content is worthy of having their work seen.

With that idea in mind, we began the America's Best Emerging Poets series, in an effort to find and promote the best up-and-coming poets on a state-by-state basis. At the end of the year, we will invite five poets from each state to contribute to a book showcasing the best emerging poets in the country, and from there, we will offer one poet our first solo book deal. To make these selections, we will rely heavily on reader reviews, so if there are any poems within this book that you particularly enjoy, please give them a mention in your Amazon review.

Now that you know a bit about how this series came to be, we'd like to thank you for taking the time to explore this edition to the America's Best Emerging Poets series. We hope you enjoy this publication, and we look forward to hearing your thoughts regarding how, together, we can build the publishing house of the future.

-the Z Publishing Team

Thoughts, Reflections, and Stream of Consciousness

When you are the nut in the nutshell you know of no other reality. You are surrounded, consumed, in the dark.
You can't see just how small, how contained, your problem is because your entire world is that problem.

– Erin McInerney

(I Feel) Nuts
Erin McInerney

When viewed from the outside,
things are simple.
Go here, do that, feel this. All things condensed can be into that
single idiom:
In a nutshell.

It implies something contained, clean, simple. And from the outside,
a nut in a nutshell is just that. It is simply a minuscule part of a much
larger, far more complex world.
But this is just outside the nutshell.

When you are the nut in the nutshell you know of no other reality.
You are surrounded,
consumed,
in the dark.
You can't see just how small, how contained, your problem is
because your entire world is that problem. And only once the shell is

cracked

does any nut realize there was something more.

Take a Walk
Steven T. S. Follmer

Take a walk within your mind.
Years will pass as blurry vintage photos,
some crumpled and torn, others framed.
Some think they will be laid out, neat
and organized like a scrapbook, but they
lay contorted, mashed together
like a car accident. Don't pause
with your camera to try and create art
from the wreckage or you will be consumed

within it, wasting what precious time
you have left. Ignore the messy heap
of hues and tints and move forward at a jog.
Deep into the journey, a wilderness
will erupt before your eyes, and the world
evaporates around you. At its edge,

thick trunks line the horizon in front
of you well beyond your sight.
A deep shaded canopy stretches
above you waving its creaking limbs,
floating in the endless sea of green. Be cautious
upon entering, but do not hesitate.
Wait too long and the sky will collapse

above you washing away the trees.
One step in, the night will travel with you,
its footsteps muffled by the padded moss
along the ground. Two steps in, the night
will leave you drowning among the trees.
Bump and scrape your way, stumble
over thick roots, knock into low-hanging branches,
and make it back to light. A breaking light

in the darkness will guide your footsteps

to a clearing, vast in land and emptiness.
A tower stands at its end, reaching
past the clouds, a monolith as black as space
without its stars, with crags deep into its core
scratching around its sides. Beyond the monolith
in its shadow hides a trench. Across it stretches

a tattered bridge, perched above a rotting ladder.
If you try to return from where you came,
the black of the trench will surround you,
pushing you against the monolith, nowhere
left to turn. Dare across the gap,
or delve deep into the darkness.

Losing Myself
Leah Dix

There was a time when I was young
There was a time when I was smart
There was a time when my heart was pure
There was a time when my mind was mine

I am now older
I am now ignoring what is right
My heart is now not so pure
My mind is now not so much mine
But someone's that I don't recognize

I have become someone who isn't me
My thoughts aren't mine
My heart's desires are those of the flesh
My soul longs for me to feed it
But I continue to ignore it

Who am I?
Where did the girl I used to be go?
I am losing myself to the desires of the flesh.
Am I too far down the path to turn around?
Where is the person I claim to be?

Hanging
Rose Simonson

The house feels heartless as I step inside. The flashlight in my palm
scans the darkened corners of the house
sweeping the mysteries they hold gently into my mind. I am almost
hoping for something scary, but more so, I am
longing for answers.
What happened to my family?

There are
abandoned bowls left with dried dinners half eaten. The chairs are
keeled over; it was all
abandoned behind when they ran. The books are barely
hanging on the shelves, and the fridge
strangles the smell of rotting jars and indistinguishable foods. The
windows have been beaten and the bedrooms
stripped of the safety that they once contained.
What happened to my family?

I hear a faint drumbeat
echoing from the basement as I near the stairs. Afraid and curious, I
slide my hand down the railing. My feet
dropping to the sound of the rhythm, I
descend. My flashlight
stutters and gives a last breath. My eyes
submerge themselves in the consuming darkness. My lips
drink the taste of fear from the air.
They are here.

What happened to me?

Smokestacks
Keegan M. Gormally

Slogging over the railroad tracks to
a broken-down Public Works truck,
the smokestacks, I resent their fumes,
the horn attached to it whistles for lunch, breaks, this end-shift
siren jostles the breakroom, homemade cookies inside
crumbled and pieced apart like goods
damaged in delivery, the tune calling
pause, nestling into cabbie hats, old sock-hop shirts, faded denim
pants,
worn warehousemen in street clothes.
I listen to the stories of my partner
just between the full changing room and foreman's office.
His face rests in the morning sun
and asks me what I think about the fact that he was born with one
kidney.
"Is that congenital?" I ask.
"No, man, I just told you, it's my kidney."
The chirp from the smokestack siren rings out,
this whistle by these tall branchless trees breaks our rest,
echoes out, brings us through the field
of a timesheet, my summer working overtime for textbooks,
in the mirror, I scan my face like a chipped barcode at the checkout
line
trying to get a clear read, over and over, at least it's temporary, I say,
over and over.

On the Nanjing Metro Platform
Alyssa Cokinis

Thank you for trying,
or maybe you weren't,
to talk to me.

Thank you for assuming
I'm not here blindly—
I'm here to learn how to be
surrounded by difference.

Thank you for asking
if I knew what way
the metro was heading—
that's what you were
asking, right?

I think I knew. What
you said, but I froze
up, the "affective filter" was high,
and I didn't know
how to tell you anything but
对不起
I'm sorry,
there's still a big hole
between us.

I'm still learning.

Pink Strawberries
Katie Rejsek

You, an easy sweetheart
you fabric softener
smoothie of illuminate
moon.
Mud and clean fleece sheets
I can't freeze the
strawberries
or they will lose their
fresh
taste
freshly picked
from you and
the golden sound of bees
popping pink chrysanthemums humming around
porch swings
around strawberries bleached
bleached strawberries who bleached
who bleached the strawberries?
I must know now
the picture is ruined.
The strawberries have been pinked
the frame fell to the ground and broke apart a
snapped
rope
worn down without notice.
I slurp in
a hypochlorite breath
before every
word.
I am brought back by a balloon
whose shadow has been touching the ground the whole time
this whole time
this whole
time.

stalk and stone
Bryan F. Flavin

i'm in iowa the early violet night vague autumn luster
i'm in beirut lit homes across the high hill bank grounded stars
snug farm rows and sidewalk corn vendors and chilling december
ancient cedar trees and multilingual shawarma signs and humid july
between the two is morning and evening and continents and seas
and ocean and storms
and blue skies and civilization
the world is too big and too small
in eight hours the sun sets in iowa low and earnest on the river as it
did in beirut orange
and elusive luster on the sea last night
eight hours between iowa cricket ensembles across the starry night as
i struggle to order
juice in beirut from the vendor bordering the fruit field
in iowa i see the sway of wooden porch swings at the house by the
latent four-way
in beirut the men sit in plastic fold-ups on the side street pavement
outside the shop
the world is too big and too small
i tear a sliver of wheat stalk and place it under my wet lip and smile
wide
i approach the sea and find a smooth glazed stone and place it in my
pocket
and between stalk and stone is morning and evening and continents
and seas and ocean
and storms and blue skies and civilization
the sun rises orange violet merge and grounded stars burn the hill
and disappear
the world is too big and too small

What I Do Know
Kelly Pyzik

I. I try to catch truths in moments without looking. Like trying to catch the night bus, it will come, it's just a matter of will and waiting.

II. I'm never afraid to jump in because either you'll be
Loved   or
Hurt

        which both really feel like something.

III. I am fragile because I hate to do things I can't do well.

IV. We love the tree leaves that break up the sky the way we love pop psych articles.

IV. Not a ton.

The Third Wise Monkey
Emilee R. Davidson

"She was kismet kissed," he sighed.

Born with a silver spoon
cotton candy curls and apple cheeks
always spinning honey from her tongue
standing close was a toothache dream.

"Why was I not so sweetly endowed?" I cried.

My lips were covered like Iwazaru at birth.

"Oh, how I hunger," we whispered.

Craving, I too, was kismet kissed
born ripe and ready to be devoured!

Ancient and True
Gitali Piekarska Guanel

Ancient people's knowledge, their truths beliefs and faiths
Amongst the world they live like all surviving day to day
They know the plants, the water, sky, the thunder, and the light
They know the food and prey that lives well-hidden from their sight
They know the power, strength, and might of the desert all around
Respect their brothers and sisters, of those to whom they're bound
And know this day, this new world, reflects upon their loss
A crime for which we all will pay—the ultimate cost
The loss of faith and knowledge, of the lives amongst our friends
The loss of our families—to live on separate ends
I wish to bridge this gap created by their crimes
I wish to live in peace—as they did back in time
I wish to share my life with all those of my kind
I wish to be my natural self—body, heart, and mind

Buffeted
Abbey Konzen

Starting to suspect I am not
the protagonist
in my own narrative
Directed around to different scenes
but no authority
to act on my own
I must wait for the push
before I can move

I'm an extra offscreen
waiting to be needed
in the background
Waiting to be jumped
to my next significant moment
regardless of whether I existed
in the time
between

Mist
Morrgan Bouler

I want to get lost in the mist…
     In the fog…
          To be completely surrounded…

Lost…

Just like in the stories from my childhood…
     To travel in one path and come across something new…

The dewy grass…
     The gray overcast sky…
          The chilly breeze…
               A taste of magic in the air…

Because that world is so much better…
          Than the one I'm currently in…

Southern Fields
Adam Jaschen

Without trees or buildings
to challenge the sky,
I don't recognize the soft
features of a town,
wrinkles of streets and storefronts,
like old laugh lines.
I drive down main expecting
the great unknown lurking
just behind the horizon
but end up south of town
awash in corn and soybeans.
Without trees or buildings
to challenge the sky
I think I'd fear God, too.

Life and Memories

And I can't decide what to focus on,
And I can't unfocus because
Everything is suddenly in focus.

– Sarah DeWolf

New Glasses
Sarah DeWolf

Look how crisp the clouds look.
I got my new glasses prescription today
And everything is
So
Weird.
It's all clear and focused,
But also somehow distorted.
Everything is bigger
And in my face,
And I can't decide what to focus on,
And I can't unfocus because
Everything is suddenly in focus.
It's all bulbous
but also beautiful.
When I look at my feet
Everything is sloping upwards towards me
And it hurts my head to look at things like this
But I can't stop looking
Because I'd forgotten
How good it all looks when it's suddenly clearer
Than it has been in so long.
It hurts my eyes,
Straining to see something I can already see,
But I just have to see
When the world is so briefly new.
The clouds especially.
I'd forgotten how good the clouds can look,
When their fluffy peaks are crisp and clear,
Even though it hurts to look
Because they seem so much bigger
Than they should be,
And I both hope for and dread
The moment when all returns to normalcy
And my eyes don't hurt,
And this headache passes,
But a cloud just looks like a cloud.

fear is a sink spilling over
Ameena Chaudhry

I wash dishes while the sun dies
and think about the time I went to church
and the time I spent a week pushing
a square block into a round hole.

my brown skin reddens and
isn't anymore the soft he said it was
last night when it was all hands
and headboards and heaven.

an ashtray smokes on the countertop,
all wrong for the lungs my mother tried to raise.

a raw grain of rice pierces my heel
gold hits me between the eyes
november yawns awake, and I am so much older
scrub another loss out of a blue glass

still in the wrong body for a modest pew
still smoothing shapes in shaking hands
I should know by now which things don't fit
but still find it difficult to stand.

A Ruined Sonnet for the Taj Mahal
A Blake Bushnell

The way it rose against the boundless sky,
Marbled white painted on a canvas blue
Was enough to spark even the dullest eye,
Enough to move the soul of artless youth.
In hazy morning light, I thought I saw,
The ghosts of hearts that once did firmly beat;
In wispy morning air, I heard a call,
A song meant only for my ears to keep.
If I have any special memory,
It is the memory of that first gaze
When heaven all at once aligned for me,
And I saw deep into the soul of the place.
O, that image I do remember well,
My mind returns to it often now
Thoughts of greatness, of awe that overwhelms,
Of Sean, and the dear time we were allowed.
Did you know he built it for his dead love?
From sweet, infinite devotion it grew
Would that I could build one for my dead love,
For Sean, whom the unkind world took from me, too.
I looked upon that place with unweathered eyes,
And knew not yet what life would ask of me;
But just as it once moved my innocent side,
It now moves wiser eyes that have sorrow seen.
While years do surely go so swiftly by,
My mem'ries of that place have not yet grayed
And just as the Shah's love will ne'er be lost to time,
So I hope too that Sean's eternal summer will not fade.

Just
Rachel Buckner

Just unearth the toxic tale
birthed from the archives of your fear
Your fingertips unravel like the notion of years past
Deep in the cracks of your skull, we burrow

Just shun the tedious tap
Beads of sweat spill down your icy shoulder
bleaching the inkblots, we leak from the page
For fractured thens drag you from this now

Just embrace the tangled realities
Our palms match but never touch
Let society sweep you into her rigid arms
And resolve
Just do. Simply do.

Body as Sir, I Mean Ma'am, I Mean Sir
Jo Teut

The first time—O'Hare
between San Francisco and Sioux City
Manchu Wok
noon
and he was tired, apologizing.

The last time—Brass Tap—Happy Hour
me and the gang
and that apology looked more like a lemon drop
and an *I'll never do it again.*

In between I lose count
of the translations
here butch there twink
here lesbian there dyke
here legal there liar
here "gender nonconforming"
there "I mean, what are you?"

Lugones tells me they attempted to colonize my mind
my body into a gender
I do not conform. They fail this time.
#translivesmatter. They win this time.
Is this playfulness?
Did someone have to die?

My body says
be you
and the phantasmal thoughts say,
speak deeper bind tighter looser clothing work out trim up
hide
those confusing parts
before they are mistranslated
again.

Whoever said hide and seek was for children
has not traveled between these borders.

But We See Fine

Kayla Krull

High cheekbones
Supple red lips
Shapely
Downcast eyes—

My scream echoes and continues.
There is no rescue from
this cursed cup. Yet deemed unworthy
to touch even this, but

I am worthy to clean everything up,
step into your home, polish silver, dust, vacuum
as scum, vermin, dumb, unintelligent, yet escaping.
Yes'um I may say but

I alone carry the ability to sustain life.
You demand and enforce:
My wife will cook and clean. Do all I say. Have no brain. Yet
dumb is pathetic and unattractive.

Aren't we beyond demeaning?
We've split by gender, race, facial features, color—
Don't my tiny green eyes see the same world?
We insist on zipping up

against any other. We remove ourselves
via space and tech. We choose
locked in a ceramic canister. My but
haven't you given up yet?

The Real Christmas Spirit
Bailey Rickels

Snowflakes drift among
the howling wind, landing
on our front porch. Family from
far away is coming to stay.
Nose pressed to the
window making smudges
on the glass. Anticipating the
 excitement of their arrival.

Grandma brings lipstick
 kisses, and her famous
fruitcake that crunches
beneath my teeth.
Bless her soul, she's getting old
I'll eat it anyway.

Auntie Jo only brings one gift.
Pretty pennies don't come by
being a mediocre artist.
I don't expect much but
the wrapping paper still crinkles
at the touch of my fingers when
I tear it open with glee.
A hand me down shirt—

I'll say thank you anyway.

We don't have it all
but really we do.
Christmas isn't
fruitcake or
a crappy gift.
It's love and faith
and family all wrapped up in one.

Acrylic Ramblings
Catherina Narigon

"I prefer sadness to emptiness,"
she tells me.
"Misery feels like velvet and the smell of a candle when you blow it
out."

I have an awful habit
of disregarding what other people are feeling.
Their worlds are holistic
and fit together without the extensive use of superglue.
My days are brushstrokes on different canvases
and I'm not much of a seamstress.
The last time I tried to iron it all together,
I burned a hole through my favorite painting.

Some mornings are brighter than others.
Yesterday was full of reds and blues
in a bold way that edged on abrasive.
It was hungry for tonal variation
and a certain uniformity that it would never be able to possess.
Other mornings, I wake up wishing I were color-blind.
I think that would hold some amount of poignant irony,
and maybe if my pieces were just a little bit more broken
I could find new ways to patch the tears in my fabric.

I have trouble responding when I'm asked about my life,
I'm not sure if I should categorize it as impressionism or pointillism.
I want the viewers to believe that it has some sort of reasoning;
that the colors I choose fulfill a purpose
and fit into a context.
With enough technical terminology,
I manage to convince a few that they are witnessing something brilliant.

I use the argument
"Anything can be art,"
and that helps me sleep at night.

Rosemary
Rob Petrie

There are times I need to remember.
I crawl back into dust and clutter
Where I keep everything I have known.
It's comfortable here.
There's a picture on a shelf of a tree.
I know this place. I am four and I wonder
How much older is the tree than me?
There is a worn-white crease up the trunk,
And fingerprints where the leaves used to be.
I know no more what the tree looks like.
Each remembrance is an injury.
So I tell myself it's the ash out my window,
But it is not nor will it be.
Each moment here is a mutilation,
And I redraw the pictures as best I can
While singing to myself:
Will there be a day
That the flesh gives way
To the wooden leg
So the pirate is the peg?
Leave the picture on the shelf,
Let it gather its dust, it is a better fate.
Nostalgia has violent hands.

Symptoms of Change
Katelyn Storey

Sometime, after the last sweltering
day of September has gone,
after the wild geese have clutched
the prairie grasses for the final time and
crabapple trees have turned
a brilliant crimson hue,
I imagine running alongside
the yellow lines of the pavement.

Past the solitary campsites with a
thin layer of frost, past the
abandoned farmhouse that leaks
golden light through
its rafters, down to the edge
of the sand. With its murky
water and scraps of fishing
line, evidence the summer
has drawn her pregnant curtains.

The first few months after you left
I wanted to be a martyr.
I thought I deserved all the suffering I could feel.
The pounding repetition of my feet
and grinding noise of late summer
roadwork were a welcome diversion.
Now the yellow lines of the pavement
are falling behind me.

Chatoyant
Jessica Luke

If I rolled it down the hall
I don't know if it would stick in the doorframe
or
roll right back to me.
These rooms have uneven floorboards.
This house has settled badly.

The cynosure of my love has had the luster of a d20
"If you swallow it, it will kill you,"
Can be said of pretty much anything
the bubblegum pink of a Paper Mate eraser
the effervescent allure of bath salt rock candy

A sour strawberry Ring Pop
that shatters between my back teeth.

A diamond she bought in a drug store
(Maybe from a vending machine.)

A question shaped like a promise
on a city park tire swing.

A ring he never pulled out of his pocket
A midnight airport where I didn't kiss him
Not like he wanted.

A glass marble in a Walmart parking lot, 1998
Sweaty, sticky-fingered, and starving
Bulging against the waistband of my saddle pants
I picked it up off the July asphalt and popped it in my mouth.

Family and Friends

I stroked your short, coarse hair graying
from age as you took your final breath.
And although you are gone,
there will always be a spot for you in my heart,
man's best friend.

– Michelle Stallard (Voelker)

The Light to My Darkness
Natasha Clawson

My best friend is the one who keeps
Me from drowning when the waves get
Rough. She also keeps me from the
Nightmares when they keep me up.
When it's dark in my world, she is the
Light who keeps me smiling even when
It's not alright.
Friends can turn into family but family can
Already be friends. The one who's in my
Family I can call my best friend. The one
Who keeps me safe when darkness arises,
I am thankful she is there to make it go away,
And to always be there in life to make it amazing.

Man's Best Friend
Michelle Stallard (Voelker)

When we first met, you were just a little ball of fur. I would
have never thought how much you could have changed my life.
In the winter, my sister would dress you
up in Grandpa's vest and hold onto your tail so you could
pull her around our ice skating rink.
You loved jumping on little air bubbles
under the surface to crack through the
ice like a fox jumping in the snow.

I remember how you loved treats
and you would always come running when
you heard me call your name.
We had the best of times. I had loved you so much
and always will.

I remember when I would leave for school; you would always see
me off. We were both sad to be separated—
thirteen years is quite some time together.
Mum would always ask you, "Where's Michelle?" You knew me by
name.
You would search all over the farm.
Of course, I would be nowhere to be found,
but you always knew that I'd come back
no matter how long I was gone.

You'd always run up to greet me
panting and wagging your tail. But this
time was different. You were
waiting for me to come home so you could see me
one last time.

I sat next to you for hours, comforting you, bringing you
water that you would not drink. It hurt me to see
you like this, once so full of life. Now just
lying in the straw unable to move, sorrow-filled eyes

staring off into the distance
at the white snow falling past the barn doors.
"Close your eyes, and you can go outside,"
I whispered, choking back the tears.

I stroked your short, coarse hair graying
from age as you took your final breath.
And although you are gone,
there will always be a spot for you in my heart,
man's best friend.

Rainbow Babies
Courtney Snodgrass

My great-grandmother suffered
her first miscarriage at the age
of 17, three months after a man
forced himself inside of her.
She swore to never have sex again
until she could bear the pain of
blood between her legs after
giving birth to a placenta rather than
losing her virginity or losing a child.
She met my great-grandfather two years
later and married in a small white chapel.

A honeymoon and a year later,
my Nana was born, the first child
in the family tree my great-grandmother
swore to protect a blonde-haired, blue-eyed
little girl with every cell in her body
until she learned to fight off men and the
pain of losing a baby's heartbeat before
being allowed to name them.

Nana lost two babies before the birth
of my mother; and after my mother,
Nana breathed life to another little girl.
Two sisters grew up, playing make-believe
in a makeshift kitchen built out of boxes
brought home from the grocery store.

My mother's sister lost her first baby
at the age of 23, a year after marrying
her husband and trying for eleven months
to conceive a tiny fetus.

My mother birthed a child into this world,
still to the touch when his heartbeat was lost

46

too far into her pregnancy.

To think a woman in my family could carry a baby
Full-term, the first time, was silly but my mother tried.

I was born, kicking and screaming, three years later
when my mother finished the worst of her grieving.

She told me she cried both tears of joy and sadness
when the doctor carried me to her bare chest with a pink hat.

I never understood why she cried until I held a small white stick
in my trembling fingers, a plus sign staring back at me

and the rest of my house, absent of children.

Love, Romance, and Heartbreak

Many lines have been crossed.
We look back as they touch the sunset,
But always one wall between us.
We talk while peering over its ledge.

– Simon Gott

The Sound of Someone Leaving
Clara Trippe

You're something beautiful, I swear to God.
That's my first memory of you: something beautiful,
heading in the opposite direction.

There is a canal where I live here, with a small
waterfall, and if you stand nearby and listen,
you will be lost to it, just the sound of falling.

There is a feeling, a second stretched across
your brain, sticky hot and glowing.
It would be nice to be happy, yes, but it
would also be nice to be spectacular,
ancient and ungodly.

There was a night my friend's father put a
blowtorch next to her lips, and she blew
moonshine into a cloud of red. The fire
uncurled through the air like a ribbon being untied.

This morning I woke up early to watch a sunrise
so soft I hardly even noticed it was happening.
The day just rolled onto me, and all of a sudden,
there was light on the water.

You won't see these things, I can only tell you:
they were more beautiful than you. They were right
in front of me, and I could hold them, each aching second:
the whole world an exhalation, a peace-be-with-you,
a story that gets told through centuries.

Pillows
Grace Lloyd

In the silent moments before
your eyelids close across azure irises
you smile.
It's beautiful: the way
your mouth parts against the cobalt pillowcase
and your fingers bite the woolen quilt.
I wonder as your eyes swerve beneath those lids
what film plays in the dark of your unconscious?
Do you see my face, plastered
against the back wall of your mind,
feel some sleeping memory of my fingers
or my lips lightly brushing your own?
I want to touch your eyelids,
gently, kiss them with my fingertips,
wake you with my touch,
disturb your peace with my affection.
I am sixteen, smitten, uncertain.
But I resist.
Instead, I prop chin on palm,
elbow piercing the mattress,
and admire you asleep beside me
until exhaustion weakens me
and gravity drags my own eyelids shut,
enveloping me in sleep alongside you,
and the very last thing I see
is the mountain range of sheet folds
burying your face,
burying us.

Basement

Jacob Chauss

I write you love poetry in my basement apartment under the bare
bulb
Don't tell the government about my plans
To drink our love from mason jars is against their ideas
And that just seems wrong to me and my Twitter followers
They have their Burger King, why can't we have it our way?
I want to skip my capitalist retail job
To sit under a tree and meditate on your podcast
It was the one you made with me in the rain
So the last hour is kind of scratchy
But I still think our ideas made an impact
The future kids will appreciate our words
As well as learn to make vegan chili
The city is peaceful and dry in February
But I wish I had a heater
Because the winters get cold without you
And I lost my body pillow of the J-pop star.

Field of Reeds
Mar von Zellen

She wears a gaggle of punch pearls around her neck,
harpoon needles in each lobe, bones a colossus of tin-cast
cunning, a knife for a kiss.

Kiss her and you open to two fates, particle or wave.
As particle she grips your dollop of a soul, laughs
voids into it, greases your apex with her iron lacework knuckles.

You fall. But within the skittering of unannounced shock
glances your eye to her eye and you realize you have seen
a woman full of killing.

A mouth packed with claws to rip fluid the tyrant
who catcalls as though at a constant catwalk in the lucid
gray street, an all-star dog bent on marking the lawn.

No words cross her lips for you. She's well-versed in the silent
treatment, with which she plants a middle finger
on each grin and wink and sexual rasp on a boss's tongue.

The arrows of reeds in her Elysian fields are harder than any man's
prick, the gull of her fire more harrowing than the largest ego
sewn onto the smallest incapable heart.

But as a wave, her kiss means love, if only love
trickling like dying dewy moss off a grave.

too much wine
Anna Ryden

a handsome stranger in the salty waves,
drops of ocean water slip-sliding down
his shimmering skin.

have I ever been so in love?

"no me olvides,"
he whispers,
lips like a fish as
he dives back into the gentle current.

"I never will,"
my voice slurs,
left in the residual warmth of
our fleeting romance
and the sinking sun.

Runaway
Luke Kingsbury

I've mastered the art
of packing my bags
and sneaking out
without a single word.

I've got enough Greyhound ticket stubs
to cover your hand-me-down globe
in paper-mache,
and enough miles
on my AmEx
to leave you a hundred times.

Even though our memories
could never fit in a single suitcase,
all I have room for is a
little black carry-on.

A carry-on to carry on;
a hope chest with no hope;
a box with nothing but stamps
and sadness—
I'm nothing if not
a little runaway.

Winter Without the Wonderland
Bianca Kesselring

Numbed by ice.
Bleak like cold.
Never has a winter been this dark before.
When will summer be back again?
Perhaps I missed it, waiting for you.

Darkness Glowing
Abby Suhr

Every night of senior year I would jump onto my bed with the joy of
a child
Flipping off the light switch and launching myself to the other side of
the room
My focus was on the stars, tacked to the wall and blurry without my
glasses
Sometimes my knees would hit the metal frame in the darkness, and
I would stumble
But a step back meant another chance at the perfect takeoff
Landing on the creaky mattress of a dorm bed, the stars gazed down
at me as I
pondered them
Trying to make constellations out of the madness
I have found that this is what it is like to love
You know the goal, but the pathway there can be nearly impossible
What you thought you knew is black, a clean slate, a starting over
It may take a few tries before you get it right
And even then the result might not be the way you imagined or
remembered it
Although the pinpoints of light on my wall remain fixed
The things they represent turn round and around and around and
around trying to
confuse me
And still, I manage to fall asleep beneath them night after night
The fading yellow glow pulls me to slumber, and I wonder
If the journey from the light switch to bed is my road to love, then
what exactly is the destination?
No matter how much light the stars drink up, they will always
become as they were
before
My love for you was like this
We poured hours into each other until I lost myself in you
Each time the fire grew dimmer we stoked it with just enough to
keep it going
But soon missed calls, ignored texts, and time apart added up

The light began to fade, and no one moved to fix it
I continue to jump on my bed every night with the joy of a child
The difference is that now I know
As beautiful as glow-in-the-dark stars are and no matter how long they glow, they will
always return to the dark

I need to tell you how
Nikol Sustrova

I need to tell you how
every evening I find myself
humming the same melody
of lost words and broken
syllables. How when I become
the instrument of our past
I gulp until my tongue is
swollen and becomes
an obstacle in my mouth
how when I open my eyes
after a night of dreamlike
discourse I find your name
on the tip of that same
swelling tongue
and how when I touch it,
I cannot feel it. Looking into
an old mirror that makes my
face look fatter and happier,
I stick out that dark red muscle
and I keep staring at it until
darkness finally descends on my
shoulders, my breasts, and my belly.
Then I lead another conversation
with my dreamless self, saying
difficult words in difficult languages
in a vain hope:
if I silence my tongue, I may
silence the tides of confusion—
the moonwalk of my mind.

After the Fight

Marisa Donnelly

When I wake up quarter past five,
and your arms are strewn across the pillow
like flower stems after a rainstorm, I count
the stray hairs of your mustache, watch
your chest twitch and think how much I love you
when you are silent.

Copestones
Simon Gott

Many lines have been crossed.
We look back as they touch the sunset,
But always one wall between us.
We talk while peering over its ledge.
Neither of us ever acknowledging its bricks,
nor how hard we strain just to be there.
Years of stones have built these odds
and either side we've remained.
Because one day I might pull down a brick
and I'll hope to see you on the other side,
doing the same.

Confinement
Nora Felt

The last time I was in this city,
I think there were less children,
there were definitely less children.

we've gotten young again.

Everything felt sadder then,
the way the clouds hung
how the buildings touched each other,
uncomfortably, frantically,

pigeons eating bread.

I was in love then,
in a fleeting type way,
aware of the expiration date on your left eyelid,

decadent grapefruits still rot.

It was sorrow and love,
the aching combination that brewed us,
the melancholic cup of coffee.

warwick ave

ambrianna daley

east of warwick avenue & i have fortune
stamped across the lines of my wrist.

she plays an organic drum for
us on a small couch with roaches &

tells me to walk south.
the streets are covered in pollen.

at 5am there is "blanco" from behind
the headlights & the night is long.

my wrists are covered in petals, the
ash from these cigarettes

& the scent of your skin whispering
fortuna on my neck, an eternity.

The Minx
C.R.Kent

My love for her runs deep,
my heart beats, aches, every day.
The dame sleeps, eats, sleeps,
Saunters, smiles 'til day's done.

Her beauty is great,
Wandering mind 'til she I see,
Sneaking is all I do,
While waiting, wishing, for her to say, "Me too."

Too Much Blood
Anna Zetterlund

You told me once of a man who felt he had too much blood. Well, it's got me thinking. Is there such a thing as too much blood? Is that this feeling I have for you? Is that this quick heat that rises and stays in my chest? The desire to be with you and shield you from your everything, your anything that frightens or threatens you? To prove to you that life and love are bigger than you can ever imagine, all by letting you feel the warmth of my heart? Too much blood.

It burns in me, I think, to comfort the cold in you. You're not cold with malice...no, of course not. You're kind and caring and beautiful. It's more like cold with insufficient fuel. Like a beautiful, incandescent fixture that glows brightly but winks, if you look closely enough. You give only the slightest hints that you're slowly fading. An elegant structure so regal as it crumbles to the ground.

And as for me? Oh, how I long to remind you of your strong foundation, beautiful structure. I long to pour hot oil into your fading lamp, because I know the Master of the minefields. I know the Source. So my soul burns for you. In place of you, if it could. I would wrap my arms around you and keep you warm forever. My soul weeps at the thought of you shivering, while I'm here basking in the glow. Come with me! Follow me to the fire.

It ignites and sears through me, consuming every part of me in heat. If only I can let it burn long enough to light your ever-emptying lamp. I would let it devour me before I would give up. Too much blood. My heart beats for two.

Wait Here
Hannah Garry

Salt lingers everywhere,
here in this new place.
He says he tastes the salt on my lips,
on my skin and in the air,
air that lulls us almost to sleep
as it sits heavily over us,
laden with the buzz of mosquitoes,
the crashing of waves.

Everyone waits here,
for shopkeepers and bus drivers,
for the blinding midday sun
to start its slow descent into night.
We wait to return,
though we pretend we are not waiting.

There's an ocean here, of course
and palm trees and all the rest.
I love how the water pulls me,
each coming wave
gently dragging me backwards,
then thrusting me forward
water crashing against the shore.

I wait here, too,
buoyed by the salt water,
floating in between waves.

Night comes, and I watch him sleep,
pull my fingers through his hair
as he breathes heavily against the pillow,
trace over the smooth skin
stretched across his shoulder blades.
And I'm floating again,
waiting
to be pulled back out to sea.

Tell Me You Love Me
Emily T. Swanson

tell me you love me
even though you don't,
because I live for clichés
and ill-timed romanticism
and words just on the edge
of false,
because I tear apart bandages
because I walk on cornerstones
because I miss being told untruths
as if all of your lies were undeniable
as though all our fights were my fault
as though you're the only innocent one.
I'm done.
I'm sick of being your charitable pastime
of being the girl you'll hug only when I cry
of being your girl in any form whatsoever.
I'm not here to be your broken record.
I'm not here to be your soundboard
and I'm certainly not here to be
your lover.

tell me you love me
or don't.
because I'm not a fan of liars
and I've grown too old to enjoy
clichés.

Irony
Alixandra Moews

Long limbs covered in goose bumps
Golden honey accent flowing through purpled lips
Ocean swell in my chest
The riptide pulling me under
Drowning in your freckled cheeks,
Your strong jawline,
You, a lifeguard, just stood and watched

Lonely Witch of the Heartlands
Alex Bazis

There are faces but no movement
Masks and paintings hung upside down
All this rebellious county can scream of are the memories broken like
dolls
And how good it is to see them gone

You quiz the night like a camera
Tuning, creeping whispers
Across the street are lime-colored smears and checkered grins
Fogged cars patient in the city park
Ruby moans searching through the negative light

The crooked house shifts, amid rust and rotten logs
A band of soldier mendicants takes part in prayer
Lies and honey, softly administered
To the jangled chorus who swiftly take their share

This isn't how it was supposed to happen
But it's good it happened all the same

You see them but never feel them
You taste their cigarettes but never light the fire
Your tongue is legendary for its bitter sweetness
But far too soft to grasp...what exactly has happened

Wordless motion
The crowd creaks, shadows setting up the stage
As a little green satyr plays its guitar
A lullaby, sharp as wanting

Too calm for words not sung in admiration
The whispers vanish, like the plastic stars on the ceiling
A peace like a toxic blanket draped over the earth
Followed by groans and sighs
The whine of yellowed memories seeking validation

Amidst drum beats and smoke curling around the horns

In this light I see everything
You're a broken dancer alone on stage
Bodies surround you but you can't see them
Through their glasses, you can't hear them
They claim to be friends but that word lost its meaning by the
headlights of a car

And now there is nothing
All bodies sway, the sound pivots
Notes crawl from the strings like flies
You'll sing it later, but it'll never be the same
The tranquility, so poisonous, and yet
Closing the door behind you and leaving
Police cars keeping a slow vigil
As the notes follow you like children out into the road

nothing gold can stay
Mary E Roche

we were not made to last
we were gold, but only for a moment
a glint of sunshine reflecting
off of us

you are gold
but you have never stayed in one place very long
i love that about you

together, maybe we do not equal gold
i'm not trying to say i am less
or less than

i'm not sure what i'm trying to say

i think i miss those moments
where we were us
everything was rosy and golden
and peaceful

i'm trying to say i still love you
i don't know how to be with you
but all i want is to be near you

so i write poems about the sun
you are always the sun
always golden
even if you have a cloudy day
a stormy week
remember that

you never stay in one place very long
but your goldenness does

i'm trying to say i miss you

Beauty

When day came and day fell, that's when I found you.
You danced under the wild sky,
Tattered edges twirling like a blazing banner.
A defiant shield.
You took my breath.
Movements effortless, Beauty painful.

– Dia LeFebvre

Iowa Boy
Katie Patyk

Your blue sunshine eyes
Planted beneath your wild cornstalk hair
Tangled by the wind from the valley
Twisting like the trunks of Cottonwood trees
You are the rolling hills and goldenrod plains all at once
A cacophony of landscapes
Your Norwegian sweater stretches on your arms
And I wonder what it would feel like to be encompassed in that wool
A rough, warm embrace
That lasts until the deer reappear
On summer evenings
You spend pounding pavement
Rubber to cement under the blazing glare of the sun
Grinding gravel to the beat of your pulse
Which is as steady and sure as growing long grasses
That you'll mow down with your footfalls
And surround your smooth skin
Soaked with summer sweat

I Dreamt I Missed the Peonies
Emma Cassabaum

woke up sweating and opened a May window
no perfume not yet
just the smell of damp black soil and four-leaf clovers
sweeping winds
and a pasture so high you lose the dog
what a day to be born
the red heifer and her new white-faced calf
two wild circles run around her mother
on legs that hardly know anything yet
and neither do I
traipsing up the ditch to the fence
in a sundress and cotton shirt
to watch how when the sun hits the placenta
still hanging from the red heifer
it looks like a stained glass window
when were the last calves born
how long has it been
it has always been spring maybe
even if I married in February
a lost brown lamb
a four-leaf clover in my pocket
boots filled with rainwater caught on the leaves
my husband goes to bed before me
nearly every night
but he always leaves a lamp on
I slide my barefoot-worn callused feet in against his calves
warm my toes from the chill
wondering when I will pick the first strawberry
how long will the asparagus last
you need about two pounds for soup
I hope the new calf is a heifer
born the same day I saw the first wild prairie roses
I want to come back when this spring is the next one
won't shave my legs
buy too many young plants

knotting macramé with my sister
pretending we have the patience
sometimes she sits on the toilet when I shower
not a moment of conversation lost
I've tracked mud in again
our floor won't be clean maybe not ever
not so long as I mourn my windward dispersal east
I can't miss the peonies
not this year

When Day Came
Dia LeFebvre

When day came and day fell, that's when I found you.
You danced under the wild sky,
Tattered edges twirling like a blazing banner.
A defiant shield.
You took my breath.
Movements effortless, Beauty painful.

I felt each step like a crashing wave, chest aching.
There is perfection in the unraveling; the destruction; the end.

When night came and night fell, that's when I lost you.
Lost you as you sank beneath the weight of the burning stars,
Wind tearing—screaming as it faced all you were.
Your strings cut.
Knees struck ground in defeat.
Failure shameful, Defiance bright.

I felt your struggle, shaking through the roots of my soul.
There is honor in the pride; the rebellion; the fight.

In the twilight between, there is hope
Faith in the simmering horizon
Beauty in the broken
And life in the promise of the rise
And the fall.

A Sunflower for Maizie
Emma Clare Deihl

She always found the light,
even amidst smudged shadows,
cast against cold corners,
when the sun crept
shamefully
behind bands of fog.

She rose
from the cracks
of some cobblestone street,
and tilted her head toward the sky,
when they had all burrowed
deep within the gray gloom,
after winter swallowed it all.

She remained,
clinging tightly to the earth,
as aged roots grabbed bits of soil,
refusing to wait
for the sun's careful contemplation.

Instead,

She gathered
every last fragment
of subtle shine,
strewn recklessly about the streets,
and wrapped her arms
around the broken blackness;
then,

She burned like gold.

Nature, Wildlife, and the Outdoors

The woods are where I like to roam
A safe place that I can call home
The sun's almost up, ready to play
Inviting in a brand-new day

– Cassie Green

Heat Lightning
Kayla Kuffel

Amber and amethyst
(or was it peach and plum?)
across the summer night sky—
I knew it was God
flashing light through an eggshell
checking on the thing inside
that should have broken out.
Forget about flying too close to the sun—
the stress of hatching can kill birds.

Madeline Island
Jenkin Benson

It drifted off like flakes of sourdough crust
while ornery seagulls squawked their Big Bay rants
at peach-flesh businessmen and sand lip kids.
Some Russian waiters sipped their shandy sours
and dreamed of summers worth the vinegar,
these La Point expats sing slurs rough as surf.
The pebbled shore, it forgets sandal trails
that Skokie birders gouged with stabile pace.
They track the lolling dawn; they sniff the scant
perfume of pine fire, brine, and frying trout.
Upon the dock, I watch the algae sway
along with sturgeon lake foam sousing June.

Cuetlaxochitl
Leah Waughtal

Poinsettias are raised for Christmas.
Its cherry leaves soak slowly from green to red.
Bloodshot and aching. All tender everything—

Pulling itself out of the Earth in December
like a terrible celebration.
Rising.
It's sore pink face
reason enough for mouthfuls of words like

domestication.

It sits on my kitchen table.
A dead kiss mark on an envelope.

They come in shipments by the hundreds and fill
supermarkets
and home improvement stores.
Bright yellow eyes staring up between soft petals.
I am afraid to touch it.

It is notoriously temperamental, never wanting to live until spring.

Then it would have to compete with the
tulips and lilies.
It gets shy in the summer.

It drops off its crimson
and blushes in the opposite direction,
turning itself forgiving and green again—becoming indistinguishable
from any
doctor's office fern.

It enjoys its own legend.
Blood sacrifice and dreadful.

Focus
Tricia Serres

My eye captures the icy window
where bitter cold creeps
into the heart of frozen glass.

A focal lens allows me
to see intricate branches
shooting out from the core of snowflakes
scattered, crystals of frostbitten
cloud droplets
stretching over the window.

To view the world,
magnify the outward spectacle,
inch closer to the mystery
of elaborate design.

My aperture directs
light through wide and narrow
channels, capturing delicate details
for broad panoramas,
vital for viewing
the big picture.

Today, the mountains
Lucia Holte

are unknowable, today they are unfamiliar, tall,
and I've been told it might be a while
for them to become less dreamlike and more tangible.

Does that make sense to you?

Today the mountains are bright, fierce, ready to take on the
morning.
Today they are tired—I would be too
     with everyone frantically walking up and down me.
Today the mountains are hazy,
     maybe from wildfires to the north.

What is it like being a mountain?

Today they are breathless,
today they are boring,
today they are polite and make small talk about the weather.
Today, dare I say it, they are like my fingerprint:
     similar to everyone on earth
     yet entirely my own.

White Koi
M. Jane Bowman

His talons are ferocious and his wings,
moony:
a conglomeration of little moon-
scales pulled close,
ebbing out the roundness
of neighbor moons.
He waxes occasionally under the cold and ghost-
black water,
sailing on an axis of belly boat
to turn the great cratered eye
down toward the sun
and up again.
He carries light in his moon buckets
like a milkmaid
bears the white heifering,
like a child pails a volume of cool water
home from the creek
to be libated into a tin tub, hearth-
warmed and soaped,
before pouring himself into the pure murk
of a blackness
blacker than can be known.

Crow Phobia
Megan Hill

No one knows the fear
I have of the four claws
at the end of their feet,
the sharp mouths
they use to eat and
what people call beaks.
I fear their dark feathers
that somehow can survive
the toughest of all weather.
I get nightmares of being in
the dark woods, running
away from those awful birds.
I fear their black, devilish eyes
along with their high pitched,
childish cries.
They make me want to hide.
I envy any of those who can easily go
outside with all of those horrible
crows.

Scuba Diving the Web
Beck O'Brien

Interconnected brain cells and Wi-Fi routers help us navigate the
ocean floor.

They said it couldn't be felt.
(Against the cool sand) our toes
—wrinkled and frozen—
push us forward like moon boots.
What does the surface of the moon feel like to bare toes?

We breathe through masks of online profiles,
And speak in slang
Untranslatable.

Bubbles rise to the surface.
Can you hear them?

They told us technology would only throw us on track.
But I don't fear being thrown underwater.
How would I fall?

I want to run.
It is frustrating to push all my cells against the particles of H_2O.
I check my phone.
Still no connection.

The bubbles have stopped rising from your mask.
I try to run towards you,
But even five yards is too far.
We shouldn't have strayed.
I am close enough to see your face.
You are holding your breath.
A single bubble escapes,
Then a school of them.
Tightly packed in cliques,
Rising according to social hierarchy.

You are laughing.
I try to swear,
But I can't with the mouthpiece in.

I check my phone.
We're connected again.

Comfort in an Old Tomb (2017)

Inspired by James Hearst's "Comfort In An Old Tune" (1971)
Bailey Baack

The fields root in an old tomb
without end—seeds nestled
in corpses, imbedded inside the
blood-rich womb of dirt and limb
The blue walls of our crypt
hold the air to our lungs
for a moment before
it seeps through the leaves of
our deadly mother's thinning hair
We do our best to beat it first
beat it down and beat it back
scythe it and smother it
stomp our boots into its skin
pluck the teeth and burn them
the ashes sire gold
Our stern parent smacks our ear
we, the runt of an ancient litter,
soon to be eaten by the sow
Instead of a squeal, a graceful
coo brings peace as the green tongue
licks away our residue

The Jogger
Cassie Green

The woods are where I like to roam
A safe place that I can call home
The sun's almost up, ready to play
Inviting in a brand-new day
My sneakers are laced and my hoodie's zipped tight
To help me on my morning plight
As I jog past the trees, ready to go
I spot something that makes me slow
A shadowy figure concealed by the forest
Crunching shoes on leaves make a quiet chorus
My hands start to shake, blood pumps through my veins
I hold my breath and my ears are strained
A flash, a blur, a movement so quick
Adrenaline surges, making me feel sick
Blood drips to the ground, soaks into the soil
My purpose is done—here ends my toil.

(Now go back and read this poem again, from bottom to top!)

Inspiration

But you owe your strength to no one. And you are all the
better because of the
struggle. You are grace. Undefeated and undefeatable.

– Ashton Weis

Take Me Back
N. Gabanski

I weep for a time that does not exist
I long for a place that cannot be found
I dwell on events that never happened
Take me back
Let me escape this history
Send me to that green country of perfection and imperfection
Show me what took place and allow my part in it
Take me back
Take me back
O take me back to my native soil of dreams
Take me back to my mind's eye
Where I can begin again.

Lioness
Ashton Weis

You are an Amazon, a lioness, a warrior, a heroine.

You carry the weight of your history in the vertebrates of your back, wedged into all the spaces of your spine.

You should sag, stumble, stagger under the bloodlines that strive to define you. To strangle you.

You pick them up, examine them in your fingers, knowing they will never be
diamonds; instead they are barely pieces of gravel, yet you contribute them to the load you carry. You add them to the slate on your back. You stoop further, closer to the earth, slower to the draw.

You've accepted the inevitable burden of this life, but you are strong, you are
infallible. All they've added is not of your doing, but you've taken it.

You've walked in a path of your own forging and never has it been easy, but you've never walked it alone. And you have become the diamond.

Your broke, bent, belittled frame is the only thing saving those who don't deserve it; and without your grace, they would have nothing, be nothing.

But you owe your strength to no one. And you are all the better because of the
struggle. You are grace. Undefeated and undefeatable.

A Simple Poem of Prayer
Shannon Meester

You are my father, my brother, my teacher
You are my friend, my lord, my God
There is nothing I cannot do when You are with me
And there is nothing of worth I can do without You
For without You, I am naught but dust in the wind

You are my maker, my master, my only savior
You are my hope, my healer, my constant comfort
When I have nothing else I have You
When I feel like nothing at all, you remind me
That I am your child whom you love far more than I can ever
comprehend

You are my everything, far more than I could ever say
I can hardly speak but for the words You give me
I cannot see unless You open up my eyes
I cannot feel unless You take my heart
All I am is Yours, all I need is You, all I want is to be with You

This is a poem, but I am not a poet
And all these words are plain and true
Oh God, all praise and honor onto You

The New Rome
Dakota Owens

No other city in the world has been
        Conquered so many times
No other city on earth sits at the junction
        Of two continents
Encircling such a rugged historical landscape

The cobblestone streets come to life
        With the booming chatter
Of crowded cafes
        Which are engulfed in a pool
Of thick white smoke
        Emitting from the ceramic bowls
Of sweet incinerating shesha

The amber sunset ricochets
        Off the reflective surface of the Bosphorus Strait
And for the fifth time that day
        Minarets simultaneously proceed to roar
The soulful call to prayer begins once more
        Bringing the chiseled mosques to life with religious lore

This is the beating heart
        Of the Republic
And the blood red flag
        They proudly stand for

This is Istanbul
        The Queen of Cities

Miscellaneous

Why waste money on funerals and caskets if people are going
to deteriorate into dust?
Flowers are a waste of time and energy
So is negativity but no one throws you away

– Shelby Minnmann

Detachment
Riley Morris

I stopped wearing rings
once I realized
they're less of a symbol
more of a prize

a life sentence for a rose,
grave pennies as the pension

closing my teeth on the silhouette of you,
unbelong(ing) to you

placing thunderclouds in disposable
cups, lightning
bolts in grocery bags

white livers go in mason jars and sugar
cubes in cigarette boxes

I bury bloomed flowers like seeds
by headstones

counting memories and cracks until the numbers don't
matter,
accepting the grief

does holy water evaporate?

Providence
Kesang Marisa Olsen

The goodbye brought him closer to me.
Just as I aimed to wash him away,
The remnants of his comfort lingered.

And I asked God to keep us from holding on,
Because when our colors run together
You can't tell where the blackness starts,
And open doors look like walls.

I am certain, true happiness is somewhere within
And all of him, the we that comes to be is a dark and vast ocean.
Inevitably fatal and overwhelmingly eternal.

He will never leave.
And I will never let him.

So I picture myself alone,
Sprawled out on a wood floor.
In a wide, empty room.

Van Morrison speaks to me;
Maybe I would sail into the mystic,
Maybe I will be coming home

But I see light from old Minneapolis street lamps
Gleaming through a tall, curtain crack
Filtered through stained glass windowpanes.

I know he is out there somewhere,
But I cannot see through the merging greens and blues.
I only feel the warmth shining through.
A safe distance.

At ease, I sip wine, pretend there is no world outside.
I exist as a single entity.

And I decide that if I must be in that ocean,
I shall be an arid vessel floating carelessly.
I have no extensions. I am tied to nothing.
I do not teeter with the wind,
Or sink under waves.
Controlled. Steady.

Because I know my happiness and his are not one.
I wish them not dependent on one another,
Even if they must exist together.

And I can't help but make up a different him,
A future him
One that still moves my soul, but no longer stings.

I know my visions are only wishes
Because we both took the elevator to the social predestination room.
Kyrios Christos, it is not my plan.
But may God hear me.

Conceptual Existence
Sydney Striegel

Our bodies are all composed of
Flesh and blood.
What is peculiar, though,
Is the infinite number of ways humans vary.

Everyone has a defining
Characteristic of themselves.
Short, skinny, smart, sweet,
Tall, thin, thick-headed, tactless.

But what if
we weren't trapped in our skin?
How would the world appear?
Would we feel color,
And see emotions?
Could we move with light,
And blend into darkness?

Our brains are always
e x p a n d i n g
With new knowledge.
What if we find a way
To escape our bodies?

Silence over Wichita

Alex Blonigen

the static 'round us ebbs and flows
as the radio man mutters a rosary
and the Commander sees the towers fall
Mother, do not cry

as the radio man mutters a rosary
the phones sing a digital dirge
Mother, do not cry
the dead shall be avenged

the phones sing us a marching song
the Commander saw the towers fall
the dead shall be avenged
the static 'round us ebbs and flows
O Mother, do not cry

Pairi-Daeza
Brynn Bogert

This is my gut garden, gull-wing
walled Gethsemane. Teeth till
the soil under the hills
and plant white twins
where blood roots spread
like spider-webs in aqueducts.

Catullus, loathsome,
looked like this. Bronze
broad forehead, rain-stained skin
green teeth, lip-lined.
& even he loved Sappho for her
blows & for her bones.

This is my gut garden
shed, filled with chains
that shake like stars
not stilled, not fixed,
but pocked like my skin
& pulled like bad men.

On its walls hang tools
sharp, sick, simple,
like shaking spears,
excited in the air, the chase
around the pimpled polis
toward Antigone's tomb.

Daughter, Little Lust of Birds,
you the garden grown now
& I the sow that roots in your roots,
the pig that pecks your listless
goose-grass. This is my gut growl
my useless language, guttural,

& given growths not fit for feed.

A Blind Man Visits the Mona Lisa

Rachel Reyes

I followed the footfalls,
The tumult of tourists,
The squeak of new sneakers
On waxed wooden floor,
The clicks of their cameras
Like a swell of cicadas,
To a climaxed crescendo
Of elbows, sweat, shoulders
That prodded, poked, pushed
And jabbed just to glimpse
This famed masterpiece.
I sense all the stares
And whispers so wary,
All basically baffled—
They may as well mutter
The blind don't belong here,
Standing in the space
Of the kind who can
Actually appreciate the art.
Leaving the Louvre,
I pass the processions;
Their sneaker steps cease
As they pause at each painting,
And lift up their lenses,
Snapping the shutters,
Then move on to the next.

I Know When Flowers Die...
Shelby Minnmann

My flowers are dying
    Yeah, that's what flowers do; they die
I know but they look so forlorn
    Everything dies: flowers, animals, computers, humans
I know but their petals are crinkling, their color vanishing
    And soon they'll be dead, you should toss them out now
That'd be cruel, they still have some petals and fragrance
    In a few days, they'll stink so pitch 'em!
But their fragrance remains semisweet and refreshing like the sun
    Furrow brow, wrinkle nose, the sun? The sun can't have a
scent.
It could if it wanted to if I'm eating a crisp delicious apple then look
at   the sun, the next time I see the bright
warmth emitting from the sky, it'll   smell like apples.
Argo the sun smells like apples sometimes
    Why waste money on flowers if they're going to get moldy and
                    rot?
Why waste money on funerals and caskets if people are going to
                deteriorate into dust?
    Flowers are a waste of time and energy
So is negativity but no one throws you away

Multiverse Theory Never Made Sense to Me
Emma Lane

I wanted to ask you about the time I
wandered into the backyard to find you
licking stars out of the sky and swallowing them whole because
today I feel full of galaxies and
I don't remember popping supernova pills.

I don't remember drinking Milky Way last night with
my double stuff Oreos and I
don't remember picking you up from the
airport.

*I am writing fiction, and it's all
your fault,* I say to you before
your bags are in the trunk, and you
stop breathing before you tell me that
you're sorry you called me for the ride.
*Atlas held the weight of the world on
his shoulders. Imagine holding
the entire universe.* You have noticed
the planets lining my spine.

The planets do not orbit and
neither do we. Spinning only on our
own axes we are lonesome dreidels being
sucked through broken black holes and
I don't know what to call it when
night bleeds slow and careful into
morning, and morning takes and takes
until it is day.

But I am night. And you are
morning. And I bleed light in
gushing, dreadful ways and
the sun is a star too.

It's a Small World

Allison Linafelter

Our world is stitched
together with roads,
threading in and out
through the fabric of farms,
forests, and forever expanding
feats of human innovation.
Each lane, boulevard, avenue,
and dusty dirt road all
bind the separate patches
of patterns and textures
that blanket the world below.

A porthole window
obstructs my view of
this quilt that grows like
a cottonwood tree shedding
its seeds that scatter
with every puff of wind.
I am flying above
a city of jumbo-sized
marshmallows that form
orderly rows and lines
below me, separated
only by knife-thin
slices of blues and greens.
I breathlessly watch
as they spiral out
into amoebic blobs,
folds of cotton clothes,
and splats of paint all
coating the world below.

Blinding white light
is all I can sense until
I draw the shades

of the window and
of my eyes. When
they groggily open
in subtle protest,
the Earth has pulled
away from the sun
no natural light is left.
But the bright lights
of the motherboard
cities continue to blink
and flash, even in power-
saving mode. The roads
are now strings of neon
icing swirling out over
a futuristic wedding cake
that I long to take a bite of.

Islands
Katie Kiesewetter

My wet body drips
As I dissolve
Into the cold bath.

I watch the water
Wash over my breasts:
The shores
Of some vast, deserted islands.

Lost islands,
Unwanted islands.
I clutch them for comfort.

And in this rare, quiet moment,
I close my eyes.
The image of her burns
Red on my lids.

I lick the tears as they fall
Into the vast pool
Of my own filth.

Fingers explore
The thick folds of my skin,
My hair.
Hers was redder.

Milk white.
Rosy tits.
That impish grin.

I think of the pictures
You hoard and cherish:
Her freckled skin,
The clitoris, a delicate seashell.

I see her.
I breathe her.
Clutch my breasts again.

Splash.
I awaken.
I choke on the taste of soap,
Of gin.

Tell me her name.
Are you with her now?
Is she like the rest?

Am I?
What have we done
To myself?

Absolution
Nathan Kooker

After the bull's blood, after the fat
and the dung, there is no Lavitical
method for sanitizing sanctuaries.

Certain Sunday afternoons I came
alone before the altar to oxidate
intinction drips, to sweep a host

of hanseled crackers, to rag and
rod and mop and bleach the many-
candled lamp, the porcelain seat.

And there has never been a sacred
way to grasp the blackened hand
that caused a window to be cut

through every nursery door. Dirt
Devil to sawdust, I never doubted
hush and stare, the cries of *unclean*

unclean, even after the jury
hung, even after the scarlet yarn
and the cedarwood and hyssop.

Sucker
Gabran Gray

Whisper my name
the way you did during
those rainy nights we spent
making love or sleeping or imagining
we could find a way out—take the bypass,
climb the exit ramp—and get ourselves to some
different place, one less kaleidoscopic but more full,
and always, in our imaginations, traveling arm in arm,
with the dirt, the autumn leaves, the snow, the bugs, the baby
bones compacting beneath our feet sheathed in those mud-coated
boots we wore when we fell in love; that is, unless we fell in love at the
creek, or the grave, or unless we fell in love always, before time, in that
space we can't see, don't believe in, folded as it is between those nights,
between your hand in mind, between each of the kaleidoscope's turns, through
which I can see the version of myself who would have stayed.

Case in point: the bagel slicer
Carla Seravalli

At noon I scrape it down with a new screw-
driver, brush off crumbs, poppy
seeds, dried blueberry, the remaining ghosts
of nourishment. Working here
is no burden. After every shift, I float home
with you somewhere far below,
but still in sight, like the mounds
of pastries in their fluted cups we toss each night
at closing. I smoke

to bring us closer: twelve minutes,
Blue Spirits and your wit, flaking apart into bits
of gray that lodge in my hair, which is now blunt
and short like a boy's. Now you are
in particles, in pins needling
the skin just enough to make my insides itch
when I breathe. You have dispersed, and so I go back

to the bagel slicer: the blade spins, hums
cleanly. Each circle I feed
down its chute rolls off
(my eternal softness for you) comes back
miraculously neutered, divided in two
and peachy in a coat of its own excess, as does
the next and I think how pretty to be born
of that which eats and blooms unwittingly given warm
enough water.

The Largest Cemetery in Ireland
Erin Rumsey

In Glasnevin Cemetery—
The final resting place
Of writers and revolutionaries—
One can pay a hefty price
For a plot near Michael Collins
Or the parents of James Joyce

The graves in front are stately,
Well-kept,
But in the back stand
The oldest headstones,
Ones of famine and poverty

Paved paths give way to grass
Manicured bushes and trees turn to gnarled plants,
Untidy edges,
Wildflowers peeking up
To seek the rare summer sun

We silently wander amongst the graves
Tilted and fading
Sinking into the earth—
Candles atop an underbaked cake,
Unreadable, unknowable,
Burnt out but never thrown away

And in this place dedicated
To names and histories
We attempt reverence
As we tread over a mass
Of long-dead people
And wonder who they were

Sudden Death at the Sugar Factory
Ana B. Dawn

Poor Mr. Misc. Laborer,
Quick tumble off the sweet, slick scaffold,
Last breath of boiling molasses
While the union men on break
Smoke and test
Homegrown ghost peppers
On New Guy, fresh from college.

You won't hear tar-garbled screams
While Jesus shouts anime reviews,
Sweeping saccharine dust
Off pipe mazes of thick juice,
Syrupy disaster sewage,
And bits of teeth and flesh.

Constant beet trucks kick up dirt
And swarm the factory
Hundreds a day during harvest,
Hauling vegetable honey in millions
To be washed, chopped, boiled, processed,
And sold off to Coca-Cola in a couple of months.

In the warehouse, Daryl shows New Guy
The proper way to kill a pigeon:
With a Channellock wrench
Chucked at feathery, stupid necks.
But cut it out when the White Hat appears,
Takes role before shift's out,
Counts one too few.
Oh, well.

And the smell of sugar sticks to you
Driving home, passing the beet trucks,
The roadkill, the murky flooded ditch.
The sick, verdant summer screams its last cry of green

Before winter shakes its suffocating icing down.

You must face the liquor store clerk's funny looks
Because sugar smells like human trash,
Like years of sweat and shit and death.

Come Meet Me in the Oubliette
Naomi Smullen

Clinking across chinks in cobblestone catacomb
Floor, bearing the caskets like corpses
Chauffeured in cold copper chariots
From life to death.
Slip trip through the trap door threshold in
Fertile earth, thighs open in consent
To a diligent worker.
(Charon never did get a day off)
Overripe, pleasantly abortive
Wet, warm, and full:
Ichor not meant for mere mortal men.
Bring the transfusion doctor; patient
needs another dose.
> Don't forget to take your medicine.
> It will make all the pain go away.

To Tell a Good Lie, Start at the Source
Charles Bass

When I was a kid, I would tell stories to frighten my classmates on the playground. The stories were never very scary. I stole a lot of them from magazines at the grocery store.

I can remember once the teacher asked me to stop because I actually scared someone. She made me tell her I made it up, that the moon wouldn't turn into blood or whatever I had said.

I knew, of course, that I had made it all up, but I wanted to be right so badly.

I always ended up being the one who was scared.
For all I knew, I could have been right.

I had a lot of nightmares, then, where I dreamed I was telling the truth.

The Road ~~To~~
B. J. Thorpe

I've pursued the image of success happiness all my life.
Were wishes like bricks and "if onlys" like mortar,
I would pave a road to her frame.
I tried that, once; hindsight shows I built walls.
Along the way, I constructed my own monster, too—
this bullheaded thing that reeks of failure and worthlessness;
the stench of decaying dreams.

You know, when I started this road I held a golden thread of
potential and self-worth.
I used it to guide myself out of my maze,
to where I could breathe, and the sun hugged me with warm
affection
while the breeze kissed my hair and whispered as I dozed on soft
grass.
Sleeping dreams spun yearnings for greener tomorrows.
Unnoticed in the night, I'd slip from my pasture, drawn back to
these aphotic tunnels,
I am paving my mythic promised future.

Somewhere along the way, I dropped that thread.
I guess I needed both hands to pull my feet from the mud.

I've lost my boots and their straps in this pit, but still, I keep
marching, keep trudging and building
even as my hands are raw, my knuckles cracked with fingers
bleeding, I grope;
slice my palms and knees as I stumble, then crawl, over the shards of
shattered expectations.
Still, wallowing in this ~~enforced~~ self-imposed isolation, I see window
gleams of opportunity.
I stalk them like a starving wolf would track its prey,
letting the ache of hope prickle and sting;
through this miserable, uphill murk, I hunt for meaning in
validation.

I tail each flash to road forks with distorted signposts.
Ragged notches spelling "want" and "need" stand pointing
everywhere—lost.
To move on, I've learned to want need it more.
These days collapsing exhausted seems routine;
tears, sweat, and blood dripping from my nose are hallmarks of my
ethic.
Felled and broken, spurred by scraping hooves and fetid breath on
my neck,
I garner the strength to stand.

Then I pick up my trowel and pavers, and kneel to work again.

Panic
Margaret Blackledge

Darkness coalesces
In the corner of my eye
Like tiny bubbles
Emerging from black water

Fingertips frozen
Black water like a mirror
Heart beating, ticking
A world of eternity

Note to the Reader

We hope you enjoyed our publication! If you have, we ask that you please consider writing a brief review for the book on Amazon.com. In your review, be sure to mention the title of the poem (or the name of the poet) that you enjoyed the most—we will take reader reviews heavily into account when it comes time to decide who will be invited to the nationwide edition of this series in 2018!

About Z Publishing House

Begun as a blog in the fall of 2015, Z Publishing, LLC, has since transitioned into book publishing. This transition is in response to the problem plaguing the publishing world: For writers, finding new readers can be tremendously difficult, and for readers, finding new, talented authors with whom they identify is like finding a needle in a haystack. With Z Publishing, no longer will anyone will anyone have to go about this process alone. By producing anthologies of multiple authors rather than single-author volumes, Z Publishing hopes to harbor a community of readers and writers, bringing all sides of the industry closer together.

To sign up for the Z Publishing newsletter or to submit your own writing to a future anthology, visit www.zpublishinghouse.com. You can also follow the evolution of Z Publishing on the following platforms:

Facebook: www.facebook.com/zpublishing
Twitter: www.twitter.com/z_publishing

Author Biographies

Bailey Baack

Bailey is a writer from Carroll, Iowa. She graduated from the University of Northern Iowa with a BA in English and composition. She focuses on young adult fiction and middle-grade fiction. You can find more of her work at www.baileybaack.com.

Charles Bass

Charles is a writer, artist, and professor of art. His work can be found at charlesbass.net.

Alex Bazis

Alex was born and raised in Boone, Iowa. He graduated from Grinnell College in 2014. He loves driving around while listening to music and trying to think of cool things to write down.

Jenkin Benson

Jenkin is a recent graduate of Grinnell College where he majored in English and political science. He is currently living in central Iowa and preparing for graduate studies in the realm of law and political theory.

Margaret Blackledge

Margaret is a senior at The University of Iowa studying environmental science. She is interested in public science outreach, music, and the great outdoors. She also writes science fiction, fantasy, and environmental or scientific essays.

Alex Blonigen

Alex is a student of mechanical engineering at Iowa State University. He enjoys petting strangers' dogs, is afraid of the dentist's office, and can be reached at alexblonigen@gmail.com.

Brynn Bogert

Brynn is a queer, transgender poet interested in the architecture of body, language, and place and the restructuring of each. She has been published in *Go!*, *Little Village Magazine*, *The Paha Review*, and *Ink Lit Mag*. She lives in Iowa City with her spouse-to-be, cat, and litany of street sounds.

Morrgan Bouler

Morrgan is a senior at Iowa Wesleyan University. When she is not watching the latest movie from Disney, Pixar, Marvel, or Lucasfilm (or watching reruns of said movies), she is working on books she plans to publish or writing more poems that remain hidden in her private journals.

M. Jane Bowman

M. Jane is a native Iowan and is currently pursuing a PhD in Renaissance literature. Her poetry often reflects her experiences growing up in the Midwest, her background in biology, and her love for all forms of animal life.

Rachel Buckner

Rachel is a graduating senior from Grinnell College. She primarily writes free verse and spoken word poetry that brings to life the anxieties of the individual and the collective. Her work also appeared in the Fall 2016 issue of *The Grinnell Review*.

A Blake Bushnell

A Blake is a creative writing major at The University of Iowa. Her poetry often explores personal experiences involving grief, love, and family. She enjoys outdoor adventures and spending time with friends and family.

Emma Cassabaum

Emma is currently a graduate student at George Washington University in Washington, DC where she focuses on education, queerness, and disability studies, all through the lens of the Midwest. She aspires to use her work and words to bring her home to the wider world and vice versa.

Ameena Chaudhry

Ameena is a Pakistani-American writer studying English and gender/women's/sexuality studies at The University of Iowa. She is a cat mom, a snow enthusiast, and enjoys tattoos and dark chocolate. She recently finished a manuscript of her first novel and plans to pursue both creative writing and nonprofit work after she graduates this coming May.

Jacob Chauss

Jacob is a graduate of Morningside College. He now spends his days with his cat.

Natasha Clawson

Natasha has been writing poems and song lyrics since 2015. She hails from Iowa and is a bright, outgoing, Christian woman who plans on using her gift of writing to share the truth about Jesus and to share her own life experiences to help others get through the struggles that she has faced in life. She can be reached at nclawson173@gmail.com and on Instagram: natasha_clawson.

Alyssa Cokinis

Alyssa grew up in Des Moines, graduating from The University of Iowa in May 2017 with BAs in theatre arts and English. Her writing and plays have seen publication and production, both within and outside of the Iowa City area. She is currently a drama teacher in Nanjing, China.

Ambrianna Daley

Ambrianna grew up in Iowa and attended Iowa State University. She has been published in *SAND* and *Sketch* literary magazines.

Emilee R. Davidson

Emilee is an undergraduate student at The University of Iowa finishing her BA in art and English with a certificate in writing. She plans to get a master's degree in art education and hopes she'll always be able to find inspiration in the people and world around her.

Ana B. Dawn

Ana, a graduate of Luther College (Decorah, Iowa), is currently occupied with writing, home cooking, and trying to escape Minnesota for her rightful homeland of South Dakota.

Emma Clare Deihl

Emma is a senior at Luther College, studying English, psychology, and Spanish. She loves wearing wool socks, making indie/folk playlists for the road trips she hopes to take, and wandering through farmers markets in search of weird vegetables.

Sarah DeWolf

Sarah is originally from Pella, Iowa. She is a junior at Truman State University majoring in English and biology.

Leah Dix

Leah is a 2018 Pekin High School graduate of Packwood, Iowa. She is the daughter of Glen and Janice Dix. She loves to read, hang out with friends and listen, sing, and make music. Leah will be attending UNI in the fall of 2018 for secondary education. Email her at dix.leahj@gmail.com.

Marisa Donnelly

Marisa is a Midwest-born, West Coast-based writer, poet, and essayist. She is a two-time winner of the Salveson Prize in Poetry and is the author of the poetry collection, *Somewhere on a Highway*. Her writing appears both in print and online, at Thought Catalog, Quote Catalog, and her personal blog, *Word & Sole*, among others. She currently resides in sunny San Diego, California.

Nora Felt

Nora has always written poetry, sometimes in places she's supposed to, like notebooks, and other times in places she's not supposed to, like her brother's stereo. Raised in the Northwest and educated in the Midwest, Nora is currently living in Madrid, Spain, teaching English to unruly youths and writing piles of poetry.

Bryan F. Flavin

Bryan is a graduate of The University of Iowa, as well as a translator and poet currently residing in France. His work has appeared in *Ink Lit Mag* and *The Translate Iowa Project*. He is currently taking requests for creative and practical French-English translation and can be reached at bryanflavinfreelance@gmail.com.

Steven T. S. Follmer

Steven, originally from Illinois, now a Florida resident, is about to graduate from Iowa State University with a bachelor's in animal ecology. He is looking to expand and improve his writing career, relying on his relationships and travels for inspiration. You can reach him at stsfollmer@gmail.com.

N. Gabanski

Nick is an aspiring novelist and poet. He's nearly finished a fantasy novel and plans to publish it by next spring. Nick's poetry is often based on the natural world and death as an entity rather than something to be feared. His passion lies in creating new worlds.

Hannah Garry

Hannah is an aspiring writer/caffeine-slinger living in Northeast Iowa. She enjoys being outdoors in the summers and spending the winters wishing that she lived somewhere warmer.

Keegan M. Gormally

Originally from Fort Dodge, Iowa, Keegan attended The University of Iowa, graduating in May of 2017 with a degree in English literature. Keegan currently attends and works at The University of Kansas, pursuing a master of science degree in education with a focus in higher education administration.

Simon Gott

Simon spent his first 18 years in Halifax, England, before moving to Iowa to earn degrees in English and psychology. Simon's focus on poetry led to him crafting a style that is both unique and relatable. You can currently find him in coffee shops all over the Midwest.

Gabran Gray

Gabran is an avid reader with a crippling caffeine addiction. He currently studies English and creative writing at The University of Iowa.

Cassie Green

Cassie is an eight-grade language arts teacher for the Linn-Mar school district in Marion, Iowa. She is the proud owner of two beautiful fur babies and loves to dance in her spare time. She is a recent graduate of Mount Mercy University and is in the process of writing her first novel!

Gitali Piekarska Guanel

Gitali will be studying her junior year of pre-medicine at The University of Iowa in fall 2018. Passionate about making a difference, she believes poetry is a brilliant way to express feelings, opinions, and experiences, and a mechanism for change and education. She desires her readers to see and learn from messages embedded in her poetry as they are transported to new places with every piece of writing.

Megan Hill

Megan grew up in Southeast Iowa and graduated from Indian Hills with an AA degree. She plans on pursuing a career in business and going to the University of Northern Iowa in the fall of 2018. She likes spending time with family, working at her job, and reading/writing poetry.

Lucia Holte

Lucia graduated in 2017 from Luther College in Decorah, Iowa. Her poems have been previously appeared in *The Oneota Review*, Luther's annual student-published literary magazine, and the *Daily Palette*, a University of Iowa project to promote awareness and appreciation for Iowa-based writers.

Adam Jaschen

Adam is a graduate of The University of Iowa where he now works and pursues additional studies. His work has appeared in *Ink Lit Mag* and The University of Iowa Theatre Department.

C.R.Kent

C.R. is an up-and-coming literary protege from the small community of Baxter, Iowa. C.R.'s most recent accomplishment was graduating from Iowa State University. C.R. has pursued many ventures since graduation, including adopting a cat whom he adores.

Bianca Kesselring

Bianca is a native of Cedar Rapids, Iowa. She earned her BBA at Mount Mercy University where she now works. More of her work can be found in the campus literary magazine, *PAHA*.

Katie Kiesewette

Katie is a graphic design and English student at The University of Iowa. While she doesn't write as often as she used to since falling in love with the visual arts, she is flattered to be included in the selection of Best Emerging Poets for Z Publishing.

Luke Kingsbury

Luke is a writer from the Iron Range in northern Minnesota. He is a graduate of The University of Iowa's Undergraduate Fiction Workshop. He lives in Iowa City, Iowa, and dedicates all his works to his nephew.

Abbey Konzen

Abbey is a 2017 graduate of Mount Mercy University from Marion, Iowa. She is pursuing her passions for making art and creative writing while setting out on a new adventure—to live on a small animal farm in Pennsylvania.

Nathan Kooker

Nathan is an Iowa native. His poetry and nonfiction have been featured in *Earthwords* and *Plain China*.

Kayla Krull

Kayla is a reading interventionist who uses writing to solve the world's problems, or at least untangle the messy things.

Kayla Kuffel

Kayla graduated from St. Ambrose University in 2016 with a BA in English and earned her MLIS from Dominican University. Her poetry tends to be saturated with nature because when she's not working in libraries, reading books, or writing poems, she's out hiking.

Emma Lane

Emma is a student at The University of Iowa who enjoys drinking tea and riding her Razor Scooter around campus.

Dia LeFebvre

Dia is a graduate of Luther College in Decorah, Iowa, with a major in studio art. She has been writing since she can remember and plans to continue as long as she either has pen and paper or a keyboard. To contact Dia, email her at lefedi01@luther.edu.

Allison Linafelter

Allison is a senior English major at Morningside College in Sioux City, Iowa. She plans on going to law school after graduation, but will never give up her love of writing. She loves podcasts, singing in a choir, talking about politics, and moderately tolerates writing research papers. She would like to thank her mom, Jean, and her cat, Sheldon, for always supporting her.

Grace Lloyd

Grace is a fresh graduate of Grinnell College in the small and warm town of Grinnell, Iowa. She was an English and theatre double major with a concentration in technology studies and loves writing of all types, from poetry to short fiction to novel and screenwriting.

Jessica Luke

Jessica is an expat, freelance writer and virulent punk from Bedford, Iowa. She is the winner of the 2013 Richard Caplan Award for Short Fiction, a $5 from a Missouri scratch-off ticket in 2011, and very little else.

Erin McInerney

Erin is a student at The University of Iowa studying English and writing. She likes to kickbox.

Shannon Meester

Shannon is currently a sophomore at The University of Iowa. She is an English-creative writing major and plans to study library science. When not in school, she lives on a farm near Holland, Iowa, and enjoys reading, writing, and learning new things.

Shelby Minnmann

Shelby is a senior at Simpson College in Indianola. She is majoring in English with quite a few minors. Shelby's involved with many campus organizations/activities such as Pride, Feminist Club, and improv. She's published several other works of poetry and nonfiction in her school's literary magazine, *Sequel*. As for career after graduation, she says, "I'd like to help people. If that's something I can do with my writing, I want to do that."

Alixandra Moews

Alixandra is a millennial working three jobs while also maintaining a blog at danceswithwolvesblog.blogspot.com, in which she talks about her experiences with mental health and tries to change the stigmas surrounding it. Email ajmoews@gmail.com for more information.

Riley Morris

Riley wants to share a meal of yellow paint with Vincent Van Gogh. She'd read her poetry to him and admire his artwork. Contact her at rileymorrispoetess@gmail.com.

Catherina Narigon

Catherina is a young adult hoping to make sense of the world through higher education and exposure to the arts. You can contact her at catherina-narigon@uiowa.edu.

Beck O'Brien

Beck is a poet studying journalism and sociology at The University of Iowa. They find inspiration in both the mundane and the profane, the natural and the supernatural. O'Brien uses poetry as an outlet to celebrate the weirdness of everyday life.

Kesang Marisa Olsen

Born in Kathmandu, Nepal, Kesang moved to Northeast Iowa at age 3 and has since lived, traveled, and studied in diverse cultures. As a journalist and activist in college, she was inspirited to bring light, through lens and voice and writing, to the struggles and beauties of humanity. You can contact Kesang at olsenkesang@gmail.com.

Dakota Owens

Dakota is a seasonal worker and avid traveler. Some of Dakota's writings reflect on experiences both at home and abroad. Dakota enjoys spending time in a natural setting and mixing in with the crowds of coffee houses and cafes.

Katie Patyk

Katie is a senior English and history major at Luther College. This is the first time that she has been featured in a collection, though some of her previous works have been published in Luther College's literary magazine, *The Oneota Review*.

Rob Petrie

Rob lives in Iowa City and spends much of his time either writing and acting in local theatre or gardening.

Kelly Pyzik

Kelly is a writer, painter, and podcaster with a BA in English from Grinnell College. By day, Kelly is an Excel wizard at an industrial supply company. Life is a crazy thing, kids.

Bailey Rickels

Bailey is a senior criminal justice student in Iowa. She is minoring in writing, psychology, and legal studies. Bailey is a four-year recipient of her university's writing scholarship and serves on the selection committee of its annual literary magazine. Bailey first started writing seriously in her senior creative writing class in high school. She gained newfound confidence in her ability to write. She hopes to continue writing throughout her life. In her free time, Bailey also enjoys thrift shopping, fishing, baking, and spending time with her friends and family.

Katie Rejsek

A recent alumna of Coe College, Katie is now an MFA candidate in New York University's creative writing program and works as an Assistant Web Editor for the *Washington Square Review*. Visit her blog at www.katierejsek.wordpress.com.

Rachel Reyes

Rachel is an undergraduate in English at Iowa State University. Her work has been previously published in *Sketch*, Iowa State's literary journal, and in *The Bookends Review*. You can reach her at rachelreyes240@gmail.com.

Mary E Roche

Mary is studying English and journalism at St. Ambrose University. She has been published in her university's journal and is editor-in-chief of the newspaper. After graduation, she hopes to find work in the publishing industry.

Erin Rumsey

Erin is currently finishing her final year at The University of Iowa where she is pursuing a degree in communication studies and certificates in writing and event planning. She can be reached at erinmrumsey@gmail.com or found on Twitter @MsErinMR.

Anna Ryden

Anna studies biology and environmental studies at Luther College. Originally from Minneapolis, Minnesota, Anna has found joy and inspiration running through scenic Northeast Iowa with her cross-country team. When not running, Anna fuels her creative mind with cheese curds and dog videos to produce poetry.

Carla Seravalli

Carla is a part-time witch and poet from Lincoln, Nebraska. She is currently studying English and creative writing at The University of Iowa. Her poetry can be found at www.answeringmachinebaby.tumblr.com, but her tweets are usually better (her handle is @greasycig).

Tricia Serres

Tricia graduated from Luther College with a bachelor's degree in biology and is currently pursuing a doctorate in physical therapy in Dubuque, Iowa. She is passionate about nature and the environment, running, and motivating people to live a healthy and active life. She believes in being well-rounded and appreciates creative and artistic works, as much as the sciences.

Rose Simonson

Originally from North Dakota, Rose is a student at The University of Iowa majoring in linguistics, English, and creative writing. She serves as the social media chair for the English Society and the creative advisor for the university's *Ink Lit Mag*. On her weekends, she volunteers for the Iowa Writer's Youth Project.

Naomi Smullen

Naomi is a New Mexico native residing in San Diego and a current undergraduate student at The University of Iowa. She is pursuing interests in creative and technical writing, as well as linguistics. She works at the Hanson Center for Technical Communication.

Courtney Snodgrass

Courtney recently graduated with her bachelor's degree in English and minors in creative writing and psychology. She served as her university's literary magazine editor for three years and enjoys hobbies like reading and writing, while also hanging out with her cat in her Midwestern home.

Michelle Stallard (Voelker)

Michelle graduated with her master's from Iowa State University in 2016. She is employed as an engineer and part time as a technical editor. She grew up on a dairy farm in Eastern Iowa where she was involved in 4-H, which sparked her interest in the creative arts.

Katelyn Storey

Katelyn was born and raised outside of Cedar Rapids, Iowa. She has consistently loved to read and write from a very young age and is fascinated by the power of the written word in connecting people. She can't think of a truer bliss than riding her bike on a backroad in Iowa during late summer, breathing in the thick, sweet country air, and watching the sun slowly set over the fields.

Sydney Striegel

Sydney is an 18-year-old girl from Iowa. She enjoys reading, music, makeup, and learning. Her journey with poetry helped her uncover who she is as a person and exposed her to new ideas. Sydney hopes to have a bright future and to continue pursuing her passions.

Abby Suhr

Abby hails from Altoona, Iowa, and is attending Luther College in pursuit of a BFA in dance. Other hobbies include being barefoot, binge-watching Netflix, choreographing in the studio, and reading anything she gets her hands on. She writes sporadically, but always from the heart.

Nikol Sustrova

Nikol grew up and studied English in the Czech Republic where she was awarded a one-year scholarship at the Mount Mercy University in Iowa. She currently resides in Canada, working as a front desk clerk by night and writing by day.

Emily T. Swanson

Emily is an undergraduate studying creative writing and music therapy at The University of Iowa. She enjoys finding new music and hearing new perspectives. In her spare time, she composes and arranges songs. She loves poetry and fiction and hopes that, throughout her life, she will continue to improve her skills as a reader and writer.

Jo Teut

Jo is currently a diversity specialist for the University of Wisconsin Colleges and Extension after finishing an MA at the University of Cincinnati and a BA at Morningside College in Sioux City, Iowa. Jo has also published in the *Kiosk* and *VLP*.

B. J. Thorpe

Though never considering herself a poet, Britany has honed the art of divining inspiration through coffee. During the interim between her position as an editing assistant for the Iowa Legislature and bedtime, Britany volunteers at her local animal shelter, spoils her family dogs, and embarks on various (mis)adventures in cooking while yelling at the news.

Clara Trippe

Clara is a poet pursuing her undergraduate degree in English at Grinnell College. She grew up in Northern Michigan and focuses most of her writing on the intersection between femme identity and pain. Her work can be seen published in the *Grinnell Review*, *High Gloss Magazine*, and on her personal blog, *Mouthful of Water*.

Leah Waughtal

Leah was born and raised in Des Moines, Iowa. She is a senior at The University of Iowa studying English, creative writing, publishing, and gender, women, and sexuality studies. You can find her online at @luminaryleah.

Ashton Weis

Ashton is a Drake University–educated nonprofit employee. An Iowa born native, she has been writing since she was 13. She has previously published two poems: "Juarez" (*Periphery*) and "You are not the you I knew" (Heavy Hands Inc.).

Mar von Zellen

Mar's poems have appeared in journals like *Rogue Agent*, *Pretty Owl Poetry*, *Anthropoid*, *Red Paint Hill*, *Sweet Tree Review*, and others. She lives in Prague with her fiancé and her cat and is currently working on her full-length novel.

Anna Zetterlund

Anna is a music and business double major at Morningside College who writes poetry as a momentary distraction from the stress of her studies. She has been twice published in her university's literary magazine and looks forward to potential publishing opportunities in the future.

Made in the USA
Lexington, KY
20 February 2018